Eating With A Stoma

Nicola Haskins

Dedication

*For my beloved father, Popsie — my hero and my heart.
Your love, strength, and pride continue to light my path, even though you're no longer by my side.
Every recipe, every flavour — especially cheese and chilli — carries a piece of you.
And to everyone living with, or who has lived with a stoma — you are brave, resilient, and truly amazing.*

Disclaimer:
This cookbook is here to offer support, ideas, and inspiration for anyone living with a stoma. Just remember — everyone's digestive system reacts to food in its own way. Before making any significant changes to your diet, especially after stoma surgery, consult with your stoma nurse, doctor or other healthcare professional.

Think of this book as a helpful guide, not a list of rules.

Feel free to tweak the recipes to suit your tastes, individual tolerances and what works best for you.

If a food doesn't agree with you, avoid it for the meantime and speak to your healthcare professional for advice.

First published in 2025 by Paragon Publishing, Rothersthorpe

© Nicola Haskins 2025

Photographs: Nicola Haskins

The rights of Nicola Haskins to be identified as the author of this work have been asserted by her in accordance with the Copyright, Designs and Patents Act of 1988.

All rights reserved; no part of this publication may be reproduced, stored in a retrieval system, or transmitted in any form or by any means, electronic, mechanical, including scanning, photocopying, recording or otherwise without the prior written consent of the publisher or a licence permitting copying in the UK issued by the Copyright Licensing Agency Ltd. www.cla.co.uk

ISBN 978-1-78792-100-9

Book design, layout and production management by Into Print
www.intoprint.net
+44 (0)1604 832149

Welcome

Welcome To My Journey With Food And A Stoma

Eating a healthy, balanced diet is important for everyone, whether you have a stoma or not.

Preparing and eating food should be an enjoyable experience.

In 1999, I underwent surgery to have a permanent Ileostomy formed due to Crohn's disease. It was a life-changing event that came with many challenges, especially when it came to understanding what I could safely eat with my new stoma. Before my surgery, I always loved to cook and experiment with ingredients; I cooked for my husband and my young son, who shared my love of trying new foods. After my surgery, I found myself in a new situation, having lost a lot of weight due to illness, I knew I needed to rebuild my strength through eating a healthy and nutritious diet.

Like many new Ostomates, I was initially confused about which foods I could eat. I was told by professionals, certain foods might cause a blockage, I didn't hear the word "might", I just heard the word "blockage" and it made me fear that I would never be able to eat some of my favourite foods again. But I realized that by tweaking the way I prepared and cooked my food, making a few little adjustments to recipes, I was able to eat and enjoy all the foods I loved.

Some foods that are known to pose a higher risk of blockage for those with a stoma include:

- Nuts
- Coconut
- Celery
- Mushrooms
- Sweetcorn
- Raw fruit skins
- Bean sprouts and bamboo shoots
- Dried fruits such as currants/raisins

In this book, I want to share my journey and offer you some of the tips, tricks, and recipes that have helped me over the years. While some foods are known to increase the risk of blockages, they don't need to be off-limits forever. With a few simple modifications, you should be able to enjoy all the foods you love once again.

There are 3 main types of Stoma: Colostomy, Ileostomy, and Urostomy. If you have an Ileostomy, it's important to be a little more cautious about foods that may cause a blockage. This is because an Ileostomy is formed from the ileum (the small bowel), which has a smaller diameter, and the skin around the stoma where it comes out onto the abdomen restricts its natural expansion.

In the early stages after surgery, you may find that you've lost some weight. It's crucial to focus on rebuilding your strength, which often involves increasing your intake of calories, fats, and proteins to aid your body's healing process. Eating small, frequent meals with snacks inbetween can help you reach your nutritional goals. You may have been advised to eat a soft or sloppy diet in the early days, you can use a liquidizer or blender to process solid foods. You can liquidize meat or vegetable casseroles or curries to make soups. You can even blend ready meals if you feel too tired to cook. However, it is not essential to blend or liquidize foods, you can mince, mash or finely chop meat and vegetables before or after cooking. Remember, you have a built-in blender right there in your mouth, so make sure to use it, and chew thoroughly! Cooking vegetables for a little longer can also make them softer and easier to digest.

Use sauces, gravies, cream, butter, milk, or custard to soften foods. Milkshakes and smoothies with a scoop of ice-cream are also a great way to add calories.

I've found a few kitchen gadgets that make meal prep quicker and easier. Some of my favourites include:

- Bullet chopper
- Hand or onion chopper
- Immersion hand blender
- Food processor
- Electric grater

Getting Started

A Journey Of Healing And Experimentation

As you begin to heal and regain your strength, you'll be able to gradually reintroduce more foods into your diet. Just remember that everyone's experience is unique. What works for one person may not work for another. But don't give up on a food just because it doesn't agree with you initially. Try a small amount again after a few weeks, and you may find that your body handles it better.

Always consult with your stoma care nurse, dietitian, or other healthcare professional before making any significant changes to your diet.

Soups
Most soups freeze well, so consider making extra to have a convenient meal ready in the freezer. On days when you're not feeling up to cooking, simply heat a portion in the microwave.

Keep some bread rolls in the freezer or have part-baked rolls on hand for an easy accompaniment.

Since soups are mostly liquid, they're also a great way to stay hydrated.

Smoothies
Smoothies are an easy way to boost your daily intake of fruits and vegetables, which are essential for a balanced diet. They're packed with nutrients and can be especially helpful in the early days after surgery.

They also make a great, healthy snack between meals.

Slow Cooker
Slow cooking helps preserve nutrients and results in healthier, more nourishing meals. It also tenderizes food, including tougher cuts of meat, making them easier to digest.

You can prepare slow cooker meals in advance by placing the ingredients in a zip-lock bag or a freezable container. When ready to use, ensure the meal is fully defrosted before adding it to the slow cooker.

Batch Cooking

Batch cooking is a great way to prepare for days when you might not have the energy to cook.

Dishes like Bolognese, chilli, and curry can be portioned out and frozen for easy meals.

Keep a stock of microwaveable rice pouches or straight-to-wok noodles in your cupboard for quick, fuss-free sides.

Contents

Soups 9
    Creamy Celery Soup 10
    Red Lentil, Tomato and Paprika Soup 13
    Spring Onion Soup 14
    Carrot and Parsnip Soup 17
    Sweetcorn Soup 18
    Minted Pea Soup & Cheesy Crisps 21
    Broccoli Soup 23

Smoothies 25

Slow cooker meals 31
    Moroccan Lamb Stew 32
    Steak and Red Wine Pie 35
    Beef Curry 36
    Chilli Con Carne 39
    Sausage & Bacon Casserole 40
    Butter Chicken 43
    Tortellini with Tomato and Chilli 44
    Vegetable Bolognese 47
    Red lentil Dahl 49

Next Steps 51
    Cottage Pie 52
    Smash Taco Burgers 55
    Dreamy Chicken with Tagliatelle 56
    Chicken Satay Skewers 59
    Chicken Caesar Salad Burgers 60
    Stuffed Chicken and Bacon 63

 Air Fryer Crispy Duck Noodles 64
 Spaghetti Carbonara 67
 Mini Toad-In-The-Holes 68
 Pan fried Sea Bass with Lemon Couscous 71
 Cod Curry 72
 Salt & Vinegar Fish & Chips 75
 Mushroom Burger 76
 Spicy Peanut Butter Pasta 79
 Giant Yorkshire with Pigs in Blankets 81

Lighter bites and sides 83
 Club Sandwich 84
 Chicken Caesar Salad 87
 Mini Chicken Kievs 88
 Breakfast Crumpet Stack 91
 Cheesy Chilli Dip 92
 Tuna, Broccoli, Pasta Salad 95
 Prawn Salad Spoons 96
 Savoury Salmon Cheesecakes 99
 Salmon Fishcakes 100
 Cheese & Onion Quiche 103
 Mini Feta and Broccoli Quiches 104
 Sweetcorn Fritters 107
 Cheese Scones 108
 Cauliflower & Broccoli Cheese 111
 Air fryer Chips 112
 Smashed Peas 115
 Mushroom Pâté 116
 Sweet Chilli Hummus 119
 Curry Paste 121

For afters 123
 Sticky Toffee Pudding 124
 Microwave Jam Sponge Puddings 127
 Apple Caramel Crumble 128
 Biscoff Cheesecake Pots 131
 Berry Crumble 132
 Banoffee Pots 135
 Pistachio and White Chocolate Cheesecake 136
 Rocky Road 139
 Carrot Cake 141

Acknowledgements *143*

Soups

Creamy Celery
Red Lentil, Tomato and Paprika
Spring Onion
Carrot and Parsnip
Sweetcorn
Minty Pea *with Cheesy Crisps*
Broccoli

Soups

Creamy Celery

Serving Size: 4

Ingredients

    2 tbsp butter
    1 onion, diced
    3 garlic cloves, minced
    1 large potato, peeled and cubed
    A whole bunch of celery, thinly sliced and ends removed (save some leaves for garnish)
    1 bay leaf, remove before blending
    Salt and pepper to taste
    ¼ tsp cayenne
    1 litre of vegetable or chicken stock
    Small handful of fresh basil, chopped
    Small handful of fresh parsley, chopped

- Heat the butter in a large pan over a medium-high heat. Add the onion and cook, stirring occasionally, for about 5 minutes until softened.
- Stir in the garlic and cook for 1-2 minutes.
- Add the potato, celery, bay leaf, salt, pepper, cayenne, and stock. Bring to a boil, then reduce the heat, cover, and simmer gently for about 15 minutes, or until the potatoes are tender.
- Turn off the heat, let the soup cool for a few minutes.
- Remove the bay leaf, and stir in the basil and parsley.
- Using a food processor or an immersion blender, blend the soup until smooth.
- Return the soup to the pan and heat gently. Stir in the 3 tbsp double cream, then remove from the heat.
- Divide into warmed bowls, garnish with celery leaves, and enjoy!

Soups

Red Lentil, Tomato and Paprika

Serving Size: 4

Ingredients

- 1 tbsp vegetable oil
- 1 onion, chopped
- 2 garlic cloves, minced
- 1 tbsp chopped fresh rosemary
- 2 tbsp smoked paprika
- 250g red lentils
- 1 tin chopped tomatoes
- 1 litre vegetable or chicken stock
- Salt and pepper to taste

Crusty baguette, sliced and buttered to serve

- Heat the oil in a large pan over a medium-high heat. Add the onion and cook, stirring occasionally for about 5 minutes, until softened.
- Stir in the garlic, rosemary and paprika. Continue to cook for a further 1 to 2 minutes.
- Add the lentils, tomatoes and stock, season with salt and pepper, bring to a boil, then reduce the heat, cover and simmer gently for about 20 minutes until the lentils are tender.
- Turn off the heat, let the soup cool for a few minutes.
- Using a food processor or an immersion blender, blend the soup until smooth.
- Return the soup to the pan and heat gently.
- Ladle into warmed serving bowls, and enjoy!

Soups

Spring Onion

Serving Size: 4

Ingredients

1 tbsp olive oil
A whole bunch of spring onions, sliced
(keep a few thinly sliced green bits for garnish)
1 garlic clove, minced
1 medium potato, peeled and chopped into small chunks
Salt and freshly ground black pepper to taste
¼ tsp dried basil
700 ml of vegetable or chicken stock
Croutons to serve

- Heat the olive oil in a large pan over a low heat. Add the spring onions and potato. Cook, stirring occasionally, for a few minutes.
- Add the garlic and cook for another minute.
- Add the stock and basil, season with salt and pepper, mix well. Bring to a boil, then reduce the heat, cover and simmer gently for 10-15 minutes.
- Remove from the heat, let the soup cool for a few minutes.
- Blend with a food processor or an immersion blender until smooth.
- If the soup is too thick, add a little more stock or boiling water.
- Return the soup to the pan and heat gently.
- Ladle into small bowls, add croutons, garnish with the reserved spring onions, and enjoy!

Soups

Carrot and Parsnip

Serving Size: 6

Ingredients

2 tbsp oil
1 white onion, diced
2 cloves of garlic, minced
1 tsp of grated fresh ginger
½ tsp ground turmeric
¼ tsp ground cinnamon
¼ tsp ground cayenne
450g carrots, roughly chopped
450g parsnips, roughly chopped
1 litre vegetable stock
1 x 400g can of full fat coconut milk
Salt and freshly ground pepper to taste
Cooked chopped crispy bacon to serve

- Heat the oil in a large pan over a medium-high heat.
- Add the onion and cook, stirring occasionally, for about 5 minutes.
- Stir in the garlic, ginger, turmeric, cinnamon and cayenne. Cook for 1 more minute.
- Add carrots and parsnips. Cook, stirring occasionally, for about 5 minutes longer.
- Pour in the vegetable stock, season with salt and pepper, bring to a boil, reduce the heat, cover and simmer until the vegetables are tender, about 20 minutes.
- Remove from heat, add the coconut milk (reserve a little to garnish) then using an immersion blender or food processor, blend until smooth.
- Return the soup to the pan, gently warm through. Ladle into warmed serving bowls. Swirl the reserved coconut milk on top, sprinkle on the chopped, cooked crispy bacon, and enjoy!

Soups

Sweetcorn
Serving Size: 4

Ingredients

    1 tbsp olive oil
    1 small white onion, diced
    1 small potato, peeled and chopped into chunks
    1 small carrot, chopped into chunks
    1 garlic clove, minced
    500ml chicken or vegetable stock
    400g frozen sweetcorn
    2 tbsp snipped fresh chives
    Salt and freshly ground pepper to taste

Crusty bread to serve

- Heat the oil in a large pan over a medium heat.
- Add the onion, potato and carrots and cook, stirring occasionally, for about 5 minutes, or until the onion softens.
- Stir in the garlic and cook for another minute, until fragrant.
- Pour in the stock, season with salt and pepper, bring to a boil, reduce the heat, cover and simmer gently for 5 minutes.
- Add the sweetcorn and chives, cover and cook for a further 10 to 15 minutes, or until the potatoes are tender.
- Turn off the heat and let the soup cool for a few minutes.
- Using an immersion blender, or food processor, blend until smooth.
- Return the soup to the pan and heat gently.
- Ladle into warmed serving bowls, garnish with the reserved chopped chives, serve with crusty bread and enjoy!

Soups

Minty Pea with Cheesy Crisps

Serving Size: 4

Ingredients

1 tbsp olive oil
1 bunch spring onions, finely sliced
Knob of butter
300g frozen peas
½ small bunch mint leaves
3 tbsp crème fraîche
750ml hot vegetable stock

Salt and freshly ground pepper to taste

For the Cheesy Crisps
50g Parmesan
Freshly ground pepper

- Heat the butter and oil in a large pan, add the spring onions and fry for 1 minute, until slightly softened.
- Add the peas and stock to the pan, bring to a boil, reduce the heat and simmer for 5 minutes.
- Remove the pan from the heat, add the mint leaves and blend with an immersion blender or food processor until smooth.
- Return the soup to the pan with the crème fraîche. Reheat gently. Season with salt and pepper to taste.

To make the cheesy crisps

- Line a baking sheet with baking paper and grate the Parmesan into 4 strips or circles. Place under a hot grill for 1 minute or until the cheese is lightly golden. Whilst still warm and flexible, release the crisps from the baking paper with a knife, lay on kitchen paper, season with freshly grated pepper and cool until firm.
- Ladle the soup into warmed serving bowls, serve the Parmesan crisps on the side and enjoy!

Soups

Broccoli
Serving Size: 2

Ingredients

    1 tbsp oil
    1 white onion, diced
    1-2 celery sticks, diced
    1 small potato, peeled and diced
    1 garlic clove, minced
    1 tsp grated fresh ginger
    sprinkle of crushed chilli flakes (optional)
    200g broccoli, cut into small florets
    4 handfuls baby spinach
    300ml hot vegetable stock, or enough to cover the veg
    Salt and freshly ground pepper to taste
    Croutons and freshly grated Parmesan to serve.

- Heat the oil in a large pan over a medium-high heat. Add the onion, celery and potato. Cook stirring occasionally, for about 3-5 minutes until softened.
- Stir in the garlic, ginger and chilli flakes (if using) and cook for 1 to 2 minutes.
- Add the broccoli, cover with the stock, season with salt and pepper, bring to a boil, then reduce the heat, cover and simmer gently for 5-10 minutes.
- Add the spinach, stir, then remove from the heat. Let the soup cool for a few minutes.
- Using a food processor or an immersion blender, blend the soup until smooth.
- Salt and pepper to taste.
- Return soup to the pan and heat gently.
- Divide into warmed bowls, sprinkle on the grated Parmesan, serve with croutons, and enjoy!

Stoma is the Greek word for "mouth" or "opening"

Smoothies

Avocado and Banana
Berry
Mango and Cherry
Strawberry

Smoothies

Avocado and Banana

Ingredients

    1 ripe avocado
    1 ripe banana
    Handful of almonds (soaked overnight to soften)
    1 cup of full fat oat or almond milk.

- The night before, add the almonds to a small bowl, cover with warm water and leave for 8-10 hours.
- Halve and stone the avocado. Using a spoon, scoop out the flesh and slice the banana.
- Drain the almonds and pat dry with kitchen paper.
- Pop everything into a blender or smoothie maker. Blitz everything until smooth.

Smoothies

Berry

Ingredients

    1 cup frozen berries, any will work but blueberries, blackberries and strawberries are my favourite *(leave at room temperature for 15 minutes)*
    ½ cup of natural or vanilla yogurt
    ½ cup of water

- Pour the water in first, then add everything else into a blender or smoothie maker.
- Blitz until smooth.
- Pour into a glass and enjoy while still cold.

Smoothies

Mango and Cherry

Ingredients

    1 cup pitted cherries, fresh or frozen *(leave at room temperature for 15 minutes if using frozen)*
    1 cup mango, chopped
    1 cup water

- Pop everything into a blender or smoothie maker.
- Blitz until smooth.
- Pour into a glass and enjoy while still cold.

Smoothies

Strawberry

Ingredients
- 8 strawberries, hulled and chopped
- ½ cup full fat milk
- ½ cup plain yogurt
- 3 tablespoons white sugar
- 2 teaspoons vanilla extract
- ½ cup cold water

- Put strawberries, milk, yogurt, sugar, water and vanilla extract into a blender or smoothie maker.
- Blitz until smooth and creamy.
- Pour into a glass and enjoy while cold.

Slow Cooked

Moroccan Lamb Stew

Steak and Red Wine Pie

Beef Curry

Chilli Con Carne

Sausage and Bacon Casserole

Butter Chicken

Tortelline with Tomato and Chilli

Vegetable Bolognese

Red Lentil Dahl

Slow Cooked

Moroccan Lamb Stew

Serving Size: 2

Ingredients

1 tbsp rapeseed oil
500g diced lamb shoulder
600ml lamb or beef stock
1 red onion, finely chopped
½ tsp fresh ginger, grated
2 garlic cloves, minced
1 tsp ground cumin
1 tsp ground coriander
1 tsp turmeric

1 tbsp tomato purée
1 tsp fresh rosemary, chopped
Small handful of fresh mint, chopped
1 cinnamon stick
1 bay leaf

Couscous or rice to serve

- Switch the slow cooker onto low. Heat the oil in a large pan over a medium-high heat. Season the lamb and fry in the pan for 5-10 minutes turning halfway through cooking, until evenly browned.
- Transfer the lamb to the slow cooker, and add the stock.
- Fry the onions in the same pan on a medium heat for 3-4 minutes, add the garlic and ginger, cook stirring for 1 minute. Add the cumin, coriander, turmeric and tomato purée to the pan, stir until everything is combined.
- Add the pan ingredients to the slow cooker, along with the rosemary, mint, bay leaf and cinnamon stick. Season with salt and pepper to taste.
- Cover and cook on low for 6-8 hours / high 4-5 hours.
- Once the lamb is cooked, remove and discard the bay leaf and cinnamon stick.
- Serve with rice or couscous, and enjoy!

Slow Cooked

Steak and Red Wine Pie

Serving Size: 4

Ingredients

1 tbsp oil
400g braising steak, cut into chunks
200ml red wine
100ml beef stock
1 tbsp tomato purée
1 tsp dried rosemary
1 tsp dried thyme
1 tsp dried oregano
1 bay leaf

1 tbsp brown sugar
1 carrot, finely chopped
½ red onion, finely chopped
I celery stick, finely chopped
1 garlic clove, minced
Salt and pepper to taste
1 sheet ready-rolled puff pastry
1 egg, beaten, to glaze
Potatoes to serve

- Heat the oil in a large pan over a medium-high heat. Season the beef and fry in the pan for 5-10 minutes turning halfway through cooking, until evenly browned.
- Transfer to the slow cooker with the rest of ingredients **except** pastry and egg.
- Cook on high for 4 hours or low for 6 hours.
- Turn the slow cooker off. Discard the bay leaf. Divide the beef mixture into 4 small ovenproof dishes or one larger pie dish. Allow to cool for around 30 minutes.
- Preheat the oven to 200°C / gas 6. Cut 4 round discs or one large to size, (cut out shapes with remaining pastry for decoration if you like) top the beef with the discs. Using a sharp knife, cut a few slits in the middle of the pie, brush with the beaten egg.
- Cook on the middle shelf for 25 minutes or until the pastry has risen and is golden brown.
- Serve with potatoes of choice, and enjoy!

Slow Cooked

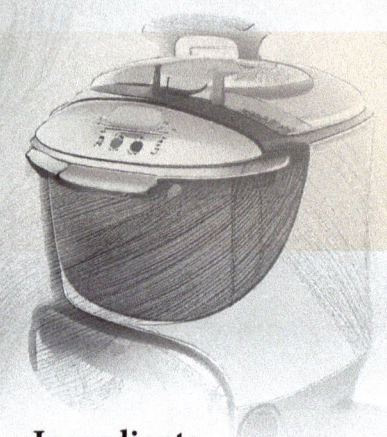

Beef Curry
Serving Size: 4

Ingredients

- 2 tbsp oil
- 500g diced braising beef
- 1 tbsp butter
- 1 large onion, finely chopped
- 2 garlic cloves, minced
- 1 tsp grated fresh ginger
- ¼ tsp hot chilli powder
- 1-2 finely chopped fresh red chilli *(if you like it hot)*
- 1 tsp turmeric
- 2 tsp ground coriander
- 1 tsp ground cardamom
- 400g can chopped tomatoes
- 1 tsp sugar
- 2 tsp garam masala
- 2 tbsp double cream
- ½ small bunch coriander, chopped
- *Naan bread or rice, to serve*

For best results, cook on the hob (see below), but still tastes great if you add everything – apart from the garam masala and cream – to a slow cooker and cook on low for 6 hours or high for 4 hours. Stir through the garam masala and cream once cooked.

- Heat 1 tbsp of the oil in a large pan over a medium-high heat. Season the beef and fry in the pan for 5-10 minutes turning halfway through cooking until evenly browned. Set aside on a plate.
- Heat the remaining oil and butter in the pan and add the onion. Cook stirring occasionally for 15 mins until golden brown.
- Add the garlic, ginger, chilli, turmeric, coriander and cardamom and cook for a few more minutes. Add the tomatoes, stock and sugar, bring to a boil.
- Return the beef, cover and gently simmer over a low heat for 1½ - 2 hrs until the meat is tender. Remove the lid for the last 20 minutes of cooking.
- Stir through the garam masala and cream. Season with salt and pepper to taste.
- Scatter over the coriander, serve with naan bread or rice, and enjoy!

Slow Cooked

Chilli con Carne

Serving Size: 4

Ingredients

- 1 tbsp oil
- 1 large onion, finely chopped
- 1 red pepper, finely diced
- 2 garlic cloves, minced
- 1 tsp chilli powder
- 1 tsp smoked paprika
- 1 tsp ground cumin
- 500g minced beef
- 2 tbsp tomato purée
- 300 ml hot beef stock
- 400g can chopped tomatoes
- ½ tsp dried marjoram *or* ¼ tsp oregano
- 400g can red kidney beans, rinsed and chopped into small pieces using a blender or food processor
- 1 square of dark chocolate

Boiled rice to serve

For best results, cook on the hob (see below), but still tastes great if you add everything – apart from the kidney beans and chocolate – to a slow cooker and cook on low for 7-8 hours or high for 4-5 hours. Add the kidney beans 30 mins before the end. Stir in the chocolate when finished cooking.

- Heat the oil in a large pan over a medium heat. Add the chopped onion, and cook for 5 minutes, stirring occasionally, until softened.
- Add the diced red pepper, garlic, chilli powder, paprika and cumin. Stir and cook for 3 more minutes, then remove from the pan and set aside.
- Turn the heat up a bit and brown the beef. Keep breaking and mixing it up for at least 5 minutes until the mince is brown. Add the veggie mixture back into the pan with 2 tbsp of tomato purée. Mix well. Pour the stock into the pan with the mince mixture. Add the chopped tomatoes and dried herbs, season with salt and pepper. Mix well. Bring to a boil, cover and simmer gently for 20 minutes, stirring occasionally.
- Drain and rinse the kidney beans. Pulse in a blender or food processor until they are no longer whole and in fairly small pieces. Add to the pan, mix well, bring to the boil again, reduce heat and simmer for 10 minutes.
- Mix in the square of dark chocolate until melted. Replace the lid and turn off the heat. Leave the chilli to stand for 20 minutes before serving.
- Serve with white rice, and enjoy!

Slow Cooked

Sausage and Bacon Casserole

Serving Size: 4

Ingredients

1 tbsp vegetable oil
1 medium red onion, finely diced
4 rashers of streaky bacon, chopped
12 chipolata sausages
3 medium carrots, chopped
400g tin chopped tomatoes
200ml hot chicken stock

3 tbsp tomato purée
½ tsp dried oregano
½ tsp dried thyme
½ tsp dried rosemary
Salt and pepper to taste
Snipped chives for garnish

Potatoes or crusty bread to serve

- Heat the oil in a large frying pan over a medium-high heat and fry the onion and bacon, stirring occasionally, for 3-4 minutes, or until the bacon is browned. Transfer to the slow cooker.
- Add the sausages to the pan and fry for 4-5 minutes, turning until browned all over.
- Add the carrots, chopped tomatoes, stock, tomato purée and herbs to the slow cooker. Season with salt and pepper to taste and give it a good stir.
- Transfer the sausages to the slow cooker.
- Cover and cook on high for 5-6 hours, or low for 7-8 hours.
- Garnish with chopped chives.
- Serve with potatoes of choice, or buttered crusty bread, and enjoy!

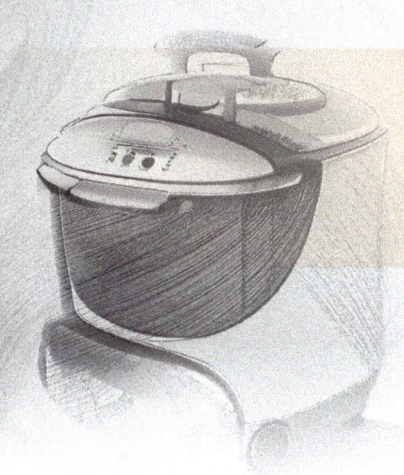

Slow Cooked

Butter Chicken

Serving Size: 4

Ingredients

4 chicken breasts, cut into bite size chunks
2 garlic cloves, minced
50g butter
1 tbsp ground turmeric
1 tsp garam masala
1 tsp ground cumin
2 x 400g tins of chopped tomatoes

1 onion, finely diced
4 tbsp double cream
Salt and pepper to taste
Snipped chives for garnish

Rice to serve

- Add all the ingredients – except the cream – to the slow cooker. Mix well and cook on high for 4 hours or low for 7 hours.
- Once cooked, stir in the cream.
- Serve with boiled rice, and enjoy!

Slow Cooked

Tortellini with Tomato and Chilli

Serving Size: 4

Ingredients

100g cherry tomatoes, halved
400g tin of chopped tomatoes
1 tbsp tomato purée
1-2 red chillies, sliced
2 garlic cloves, minced
1 onion, chopped
1 celery stick, chopped
2 carrots, chopped
1 tsp dried oregano

250ml hot vegetable stock
Salt and pepper to taste
250g shop-bought tomato and mozzarella tortellini
Handful of fresh basil, plus extra leaves to garnish

Crusty white bread to serve

- Add all the ingredients – except the tortellini and basil – to the slow cooker. Mix well and cook on high for 3 hours or low for 5 hours.
- Blend with an immersion blender or transfer to a food processor and blend until smooth.
- Transfer back to the slow cooker, stir in the tortellini and basil and cook on high for another 15-20 minutes.
- Serve in warmed bowls, garnish with the reserved basil leaves, and enjoy!

Slow Cooked

Vegetable Bolognese

Serving Size: 4

Ingredients

1 tbsp olive oil

250g chestnut mushrooms, very finely diced *(pulse in a food processor or use a hand chopper)*

1 large onion, finely chopped

1 red pepper, finely diced

2 celery stalks, finely diced

2 garlic cloves, minced

2 carrots, grated

1 courgette, grated

½ tsp dried thyme

½ tsp dried rosemary

1 bay leaf

400g tin chopped tomatoes

2 tbsp tomato purée

300 ml *(or enough to cover the veg)* hot vegetable stock

Salt and pepper to taste

Small handful fresh basil, finely chopped

Cooked spaghetti or pasta of choice

Freshly grated Parmesan, to serve

- Heat the oil in a large pan over a medium heat. Fry the mushrooms with a good pinch of salt, stirring occasionally for 5-6 minutes or until the liquid has been cooked off. Add to the slow cooker.
- Using the same pan, fry the onion, red pepper and celery for 3-4 minutes until starting to soften. Stir in the garlic and fry for a further 30 seconds before transferring to the slow cooker.
- Add the carrots, courgette, thyme, rosemary and bay leaf. Stir in the chopped tomatoes, purée and stock. Season with salt and pepper to taste.
- Cover with the lid, and cook on high for 4-5 hours or low for 6-7 hours.
- Stir in the chopped basil 30 minutes before the end of cooking.
- Remove the bay leaf and discard.
- Serve with cooked spaghetti or pasta, sprinkle over some freshly grated Parmesan, and enjoy!

Slow Cooked

Red Lentil Dahl

Serving Size: 4

Ingredients

1 white onion, finely diced
3 garlic cloves, minced
1 tbsp finely grated ginger
2 tsp ground cumin
4 tbsp curry paste
250g red lentils
400g tin chopped tomatoes
100ml hot vegetable stock

Finely sliced red chilli and fresh coriander or parsley to garnish.

Garlic naan bread to serve

- Add all the ingredients – except the garnish – into a slow cooker.
- Give it a good stir and cook on high for 3-4 hours or low for 5-6 hours.
- Serve in warmed bowls with garlic naan bread, and enjoy!

Stoma surgery has been around since the 1700's;
Stoma formation was perfected by Sir Bryan Brooke in 1952

Next Steps

Cottage Pie
Smash Taco Burgers
Dreamy Chicken with Tagliatelle
Chicken Satay Skewers
Chicken Caesar Salad Burgers
Stuffed Chicken and Bacon
Air Fryer Crispy Duck Noodles
Spaghetti Carbonara
Mini Toad-In-The-Holes
Giant Yorkshire with Pigs in Blankets
Pan fried Sea Bass with lemon Couscous
Cod Curry
Salt & Vinegar Fish & Chips
Mushroom Burger
Spicy Peanut Butter Pasta

Next Steps

Cottage Pie

Serving Size: 6

Ingredients

2 tbsp vegetable oil
1 onion, very finely diced
1 garlic clove, minced
2 celery stalks, finely diced
2 carrots, grated
500g minced beef
1 tbsp plain flour
2 tbsp tomato purée
125ml red wine

200ml beef stock
1 bay leaf
1 tsp dried thyme
Salt and pepper to taste
650g potatoes, peeled / chopped
40g butter
1 tsp Dijon mustard
50g mature cheddar, grated
Vegetables to serve

- Heat 1 tbsp oil in a large pan over a medium heat. Add the onion and fry, stirring, for 2 minutes until slightly softened. Add the garlic, celery and carrot. Cook, stirring, for 3-4 minutes. Transfer to a bowl and set aside.
- In the same pan, add 1 tbsp oil and increase the heat. Add the beef and cook, stirring, for 4-5 minutes or until browned.
- Stir in the flour, followed by the tomato purée and red wine. Return the vegetables to the pan and give it a good stir.
- Add the beef stock, bay leaf, thyme, salt and pepper. Bring to a boil, then reduce heat, cover, and gently simmer for 10 mins, stirring occasionally.
- Take off the heat. Remove and discard the bay leaf. Spoon the mince mixture into 1 large or 6 small ovenproof dishes. Leave to cool whilst making the mash topping. Preheat the oven to 200°C / gas 6.
- Cook the potatoes in a large pan of boiling salted water for 20 minutes. Drain well and return to the pan. Add the butter and mustard, mash well, and season with salt and pepper.
- Spoon the mashed potato on top of the beef mix, using the back of a spoon to spread it out. Use a fork to rough and swirl the mash. Sprinkle with the grated cheese. Bake for about 30 minutes, until the top is golden and crispy. Serve with vegetables, and enjoy!

Next Steps

Smash Taco Burgers

Serving Size: 4

Ingredients

3 tbsp mayonnaise
3 tbsp ketchup
1 tsp apple cider vinegar or white wine vinegar
½ tsp onion powder
½ tsp garlic granules
1 tsp Dijon mustard
250g lean beef mince
1 tsp Cajun seasoning
Salt and pepper to taste

4 small flour tortillas
4 slices of burger cheese
¼ of an iceberg lettuce, very finely sliced *(iceberg lettuce has a lower fibre content compared to other lettuces, making it easier to digest)*
½ a red onion, very finely chopped
Handful cherry tomatoes, very finely chopped

- Make the sauce by mixing together the mayonnaise, ketchup, vinegar, onion powder, garlic granules and Dijon mustard in a small bowl, then set aside.
- Mix the beef mince with the Cajun seasoning, salt and pepper, then *(with clean hands)* roll into 4 equal size balls. Press a ball onto each tortilla to make a thin layer, spreading the mince right to the edges.
- Heat a large frying pan on a high heat, place the tortillas beef side down in the pan. Use a fish slice to push down or 'smash' the burgers and cook for 4-5 minutes.
- Flip them over, place a slice of cheese on top of each burger and leave to melt for about a minute. If you have a lid for the frying pan, place it on top to help the cheese melt.
- Remove the burgers from the pan, place into a taco holder *(if you have one)*, sprinkle with the shredded lettuce, chopped tomatoes and chopped red onion, then drizzle with the burger sauce. Enjoy!

Next Steps

Dreamy Chicken with Tagliatelle

Serving Size: 4

Ingredients

- 3-4 tbsp plain flour
- Salt and freshly ground black pepper
- 4 chicken breasts
- 130g sun-dried tomatoes from a jar in oil, drained *(reserving the oil)* and very finely diced
- 1 red onion, very finely chopped
- 2 garlic cloves, minced
- 1 tsp chilli flakes
- 1 tsp smoked paprika
- ½ tsp dried thyme
- ½ tsp dried oregano
- 150ml double cream
- 250ml chicken stock
- 40g Parmesan, grated
- A few sprigs of fresh parsley to garnish

Fresh tagliatelle to serve

- Sprinkle the flour on a plate and season with salt and pepper. Pat the chicken dry with kitchen roll, then coat with the flour.
- Heat a large pan over a medium heat, add 2 tbsp of the sun-dried tomato oil, and fry the chicken for 8-10 minutes, turning halfway, until brown on both sides. Remove the chicken from the pan, and set aside on a plate.
- Add another tbsp of sun-dried tomato oil into the same pan and reduce the heat to low. Stir in the onion, cook for 8-10 minutes until softened, stirring occasionally.
- Stir in the garlic and cook for a further minute. Add the sun-dried tomatoes, chilli, paprika, thyme and oregano.
- Pour in the stock and cream, season with salt and pepper, stir well. Return the chicken to the pan. Cover and cook on a low heat for 15-20 minutes. Turn the chicken halfway through cooking.
- Once the chicken is cooked, remove from the heat. Stir in the Parmesan.
- Serve with cooked tagliatelle, a little more grated Parmesan and garnish with fresh parsley. Enjoy!

Next Steps

Chicken Satay Skewers

Serving Size: 2

Ingredients

For the chicken skewers
½ 400ml tin of coconut milk
(reserve the rest for the sauce)
2 chicken breasts
1 tbsp dark soy sauce
1 garlic clove, minced
½ tsp ground cumin
½ tsp dried coriander leaves
¼ tsp ground ginger

For the dip
3 tbsp smooth peanut butter
1 tbsp dark soy sauce
1 tbsp fish sauce
1 tbsp toasted sesame oil
200ml coconut milk
1 tbsp light brown sugar
½ tsp dried chilli flakes
½ tsp ground coriander
Juice of 1 lime

- Soak 8 wooden skewers in cold water whilst preparing the chicken.
- Empty a 400ml tin of coconut milk into a large bowl, give it a good mix so it's no longer separated. Pour 200ml into a smaller bowl, cover and set aside for the dip.
- Slice the chicken lengthways into strips and add to the coconut milk in the large bowl. Add the soy sauce, garlic, cumin, coriander and ginger. Combine ingredients until the chicken is evenly coated. Cover and place in the fridge to marinate for 30 minutes.
- In a small pan, add the peanut butter, soy and fish sauce, sesame oil, the reserved coconut milk, sugar, chilli flakes and coriander. Heat over a medium heat, stirring. Don't let it come to a boil. Remove from the heat and stir in the lime juice. Set aside.
- Thread the chicken onto the soaked skewers. Heat a griddle pan until hot, spray or brush a little oil over the pan and cook the skewers for 10 mins, turning 2-3 times until the chicken is cooked through and golden brown.
- Serve the skewers on a plate with the warm sauce, garnish with chopped coriander, and enjoy!

Next Steps

Chicken Caesar Salad Burgers
Serving Size: 2

Ingredients

1 garlic clove, minced
1 anchovy fillet, mashed with a fork
Parmesan cheese for grating and shaving
5 tbsp mayonnaise
1 tsp Dijon mustard
1 tbsp white wine vinegar
Salt and pepper to taste

2 small skinless chicken breasts
1 tsp olive oil
2 ciabatta rolls, halved
1-2 Iceberg lettuce leaves *(Iceberg lettuce has a lower fibre content compared to others, making it easier to digest)*
1 hard-boiled egg, sliced

- Mix the garlic and anchovy together in a small bowl. Grate a handful of Parmesan cheese and mix with the garlic, anchovy, mayonnaise, Dijon mustard and white wine vinegar. Season with salt and pepper to taste.
- Heat a griddle pan or frying pan over a high heat until hot. Brush the chicken with olive oil, and season with salt and pepper on both sides.
- Place the chicken breast into the pan and cook for 5 minutes on each side or until cooked through, and golden brown. Remove from the pan and set aside on a plate to rest.
- Put the rolls cut side down on the griddle pan to lightly toast them.
- Once toasted, build your burger by layering shredded lettuce, sliced egg, chicken breast, and a good smearing of the sauce. Top with shavings of Parmesan, and enjoy!

Next Steps

Stuffed Chicken and Bacon

Serving Size: 4

Ingredients

4 medium chicken breasts

16 rashers of smoked streaky bacon

170g stuffing mix

Good knob of butter

Potatoes and steamed root vegetables to serve

- Prepare the stuffing mix according to packet instructions, add the butter, mix well and leave to cool slightly.
- Slice the chicken breasts lengthways to create a pocket. Fill with the stuffing and tightly wrap each breast in 4 of the bacon rashers.
- Pre-heat the air fryer to 190ºC and set for 20 minutes.
- Loosely wrap the chicken parcels in foil and place in the air fryer. After 10 minutes, carefully remove the foil and continue cooking for the remaining 10 minutes, or until the chicken is cooked through and the bacon is crispy.
- Remove from the air fryer and rest for 5 minutes on a warm plate before serving with choice of potatoes and vegetables. Enjoy!

Notes

Alternatively, pre-heat oven to 200ºC / gas 6, and cook on the middle shelf for 25-30 minutes.

Next Steps

Air Fryer Crispy Duck Noodles

Serving Size: 2

Ingredients

½ an oven ready aromatic crispy duck
1 tsp oil
Hoisin sauce
1 garlic clove, minced
1 tsp fresh ginger, grated
1 tbsp sweet chilli sauce
1 tbsp light soy sauce
4 spring onions, finely sliced

Noodles
Splash of light soy sauce
Fresh red chilli, thinly sliced *(optional)*

- Pre-heat air fryer to 200ºC and set for 25 minutes. Lightly brush oil over the duck skin and cook skin side up for 20 minutes. Pull the draw out, glaze the duck with Hoisin sauce and put back in for the last 5 minutes.
- Place the duck onto a plate and using 2 forks, shred the duck *(including the skin)*. Discard the bones.
- Place the noodles in a large bowl and cover with boiling water. Put a lid over and leave to stand.
- Heat 1 tbsp of oil in a large frying pan on a low heat, add the garlic and ginger, stir fry for 2 minutes. Add the sweet chilli sauce and soy sauce. Stir fry for a further minute, then add the shredded duck to heat through. Sprinkle with spring onions, stir and turn off the heat.
- Drain the noodles, add a splash of soy sauce, give it all a mix, then using tongs, lift the noodles onto a serving plate and spoon on the duck with sauce from the pan.
- Garnish with sliced fresh chillies, if using, and enjoy!

Next Steps

Spaghetti Carbonara

Serving Size: 2

Ingredients

1 tbsp olive oil
150g guanciale or pancetta, finely chopped
1 garlic clove left whole
200g spaghetti or linguine

3 egg yolks
50g Parmesan, finely grated
Salt and freshly ground black pepper

- Heat the oil gently in a large pan. Fry the guanciale or pancetta and garlic for about 10 minutes until the meat is golden and crisp. Turn off the heat, remove and discard the garlic clove.
- Bring a large pan of salted water to a boil. Add the pasta and cook until al dente. Whisk the 3 egg yolks in a small bowl, add a pinch of salt and set aside.
- Using kitchen tongs, lift the pasta from the water into the pancetta pan, along with any dripping water. Using a wooden spoon, stir the pasta and meat until combined. If it looks dry, add a small amount of pasta water and mix it in. Keep adding until you see a little pasta water at the bottom of the pan.
- Pour the beaten egg yolks into the pasta and stir vigorously. Add most of the Parmesan and beat again until you have a smooth sauce that is the consistency of double cream. Season with salt and pepper.
- Transfer to warmed serving dishes, top with the remaining Parmesan, and enjoy!

Next Steps

Mini Toad-In-The-Holes

Serving Size: 6

Ingredients

Vegetable oil
2 large eggs
100g plain flour
100g milk

Salt and pepper to taste
12 cocktail sausages (uncooked)
4 rashers of streaky bacon, snipped into small pieces

1 tbsp of fresh rosemary, finely chopped

Potatoes, vegetables of choice and meaty gravy to serve

- Pre-heat oven to gas 8 / 230°C
- Drizzle a little vegetable oil into a deep 6-hole muffin tin. Place in the top of the oven for 10-15 minutes, until the oil is very hot.
- Whilst the oil is heating, whisk the eggs into the milk, add the flour, rosemary and salt and pepper to taste. Whisk again until smooth.
- Trying to be quick, so the oil remains hot, carefully remove the tin from the oven and pour the batter mix into each hole. Place 2 sausages in each and sprinkle the chopped bacon on top.
- Return to the oven and cook for 5 minutes before turning the heat down to gas 6 / 200°C. Continue to cook for 15-20 minutes or until the toads have risen and are golden brown.
- Serve with potatoes, vegetables of your choice and meaty gravy. Enjoy!

Next Steps

Pan Fried Sea Bass with Lemon Couscous

Serving Size: 2

Ingredients

Couscous
2 tbsp olive oil
1 garlic clove minced
1 packet easy cook couscous
160ml chicken or vegetable stock
Zest of half small lemon
2 tbsp fresh lemon juice
2 tbsp chopped fresh parsley

Fish
2 sea bass fillets
2 tbsp olive oil and a good knob of butter
Salt and pepper

Couscous

- Heat the olive oil in a medium saucepan over a medium-low heat.
- Add the garlic and cook for about 20 seconds.
- Remove from the heat, pour in the stock, lemon zest, lemon juice, and season with salt to taste. Place over a medium-high heat and bring to a boil.
- Pour in the couscous, stir and remove from heat. Cover with a lid.
- Leave to rest – off the heat – whilst cooking the fish.

Sea Bass

- Pat the sea bass dry with kitchen roll, score the skin with a sharp knife.
- Heat 1 tbsp olive oil and a knob of butter in a frying pan until hot.
- Season the fillets and place skin-side down in the pan. Cook until the skin is golden and crisp, and the flesh is changing colour. Turn the fillets over and cook for 1 minute more, then remove from the heat.
- Add the parsley to the couscous and fluff with a fork. Serve on a plate, place the sea bass on top, and enjoy!

Next Steps

Cod Curry

Serving Size: 2

Ingredients

1 tbsp olive oil
1 small onion, finely chopped
1 garlic clove minced
1 tsp grated ginger
½ tbsp tumeric
1 tsp garam masala
½ tsp chilli powder
250ml coconut milk
100ml water

250g skinless & boneless cod fillet, cut into chunks
2 tbsp defrosted peas, crushed with a fork
Salt and pepper to taste.

1 red chilli, finely sliced *(optional)*

Boiled rice to serve

- Heat the olive oil in a pan over a medium heat. Add the onion and fry, stirring occasionally for about 5 minutes, until softened.
- Stir in the garlic, ginger, turmeric, garam masala and chilli powder. Cook for another minute.
- Pour in the coconut milk and water. Bring to a boil, then reduce the heat and simmer gently for 10 minutes.
- Give the sauce a stir, then add the fish and crushed peas. Bring back to a simmer and cook for another 5 minutes.
- Season with salt and pepper. If using, sprinkle with the red chilli.
- Serve with rice, and enjoy!

Next Steps

Salt & Vinegar Fish & Chips

Serving Size: 2

Ingredients

2 skinless and boneless cod fillets
2 tbsp plain flour
Sea salt
1 small egg, beaten
1 packet salt & vinegar crisps, crushed

Chips of choice, mushy peas, lemon wedges and tartare sauce to serve

- Gently dry the cod with kitchen roll.
- Place the flour on a shallow plate. Add a good grind of sea salt. Lay the cod in the flour and coat on both sides. Dip in the beaten egg, then coat both sides with the crushed crisps.
- Heat the air fryer to 190C, and set to 15 minutes.
- Carefully place the cod into the basket and cook.
- Serve the fish with chips *(check out my air fryer chip recipe!)*, mushy peas, tartare sauce, lemon wedges, and enjoy!

Next Steps

Mushroom Burger

Serving Size: 6

Ingredients

1 tbsp olive oil
1 red onion, very finely diced
375g chestnut mushrooms, diced
125g shiitake mushrooms, diced
1 tbsp dark soy sauce
2 tbsp balsamic vinegar
2 garlic cloves, minced
½ tsp smoked paprika
1 tbsp honey

50g walnuts, finely chopped
220g cooked short-grain sticky rice
2 x 50g panko breadcrumbs
Salt and pepper to taste
Worcestershire sauce, for brushing
Round smoked cheese slices
Iceberg lettuce *(optional)*
Toasted brioche burger rolls

- Heat the oil in a large pan over a medium heat. Add onion and fry for a minute until soft. Add the mushrooms and a good pinch of salt. Fry, stirring occasionally, for 7-8 minutes, until browned and no liquid remains.
- Stir in the soy sauce and vinegar. Reduce heat, then add the garlic, smoked paprika and honey. Remove from heat and let cool slightly.
- In a food processor, combine the mushroom mix, walnuts, rice and 50g breadcrumbs. Pulse until combined.
- Transfer to a large bowl and fold in the remaining breadcrumbs. Season with salt and pepper to taste.
- With clean hands, form into 6 burgers. Place onto a large plate and chill in the fridge for 1 hour.
- Heat a large frying pan over a medium heat. Lightly oil the heated pan and cook the burgers for 5-6 minutes on each side, or until cooked through and golden brown.
- Brush with the Worcestershire sauce and top each with a slice of cheese. Remove from heat and serve in the toasted brioche rolls. Enjoy!

Next Steps

Spicy Peanut Butter Pasta

Serving Size: 2

Ingredients

200g fusilli *(or pasta of choice)*
3 tbsp smooth peanut butter
1 tbsp dark soy sauce
1 tbsp toasted sesame oil
200ml coconut milk
1tbsp light brown sugar
½ tsp garlic powder
½ tsp dried chilli flakes *(or more, if you like it hot)*

½ tsp ground coriander
2-3 tbsp boiling pasta water

Green part 1 spring onion, finely sliced
Pinch of sesame seeds
Pinch of dried chilli flakes *(optional)*

- Cook the pasta according to packet instructions.
- Whilst the pasta is cooking, heat peanut butter, soy sauce, sesame oil, coconut milk, sugar, garlic powder, chilli flakes and coriander in a small pan over a medium heat, stirring continuously. Do not let it boil. Spoon 2-3 tbsp of the boiling pasta water into the sauce. Stir until smooth and coats the back of the spoon. Turn off the heat.
- Drain the pasta, then stir through the peanut sauce.
- Serve in warmed bowls. Sprinkle with sliced spring onion, sesame seeds and chilli flakes. Enjoy!

Next Steps

Giant Yorkshire with Pigs in Blankets

Serving Size: 2

Ingredients

Yorkshire Pudding
2 tbsp oil for the tin
2 large eggs
100g plain flour
100ml full fat milk
Salt and pepper

4 chipolatas *(I use Tesco Finest British Pork & Honey)*
4 rashers of smoked streaky bacon

Potato Mash
2 large floury potatoes, peeled and cut into even chunks
25g butter
100ml full fat milk
2 tsp Dijon mustard
Salt and pepper to taste

Swede and Carrot Mash
200g carrots, peeled and chopped
200g swede, peeled and chopped
15g butter
1 garlic clove, crushed
Salt and pepper to taste

Pigs in Blankets

- Wrap one rasher of bacon around each chipolata, place on a baking tray and put in the fridge until you're ready to cook the Yorkshire puddings.

Yorkshire Puddings

- Crack the eggs into a jug, add the flour, whisk together until smooth, gradually add the milk and continue to whisk, season and chill in the fridge for 30 minutes.
- Heat the oven to 230ºC / gas 8. Divide the oil into 2 large round baking tins, then put in the oven to heat the oil.
- Once smoking hot carefully pour the batter into the tins and cook on the middle shelf for 25 minutes.
- Cook the pigs in blankets on the bottom shelf for 25 minutes.

Potato Mash

- Cook the potatoes in a pan of boiling salted water for 20 minutes. Drain well and return to the pan.
- Heat the milk in a microwave for 30 seconds, pour over the potatoes with the butter and mustard. Mash well, season with salt and pepper.

Swede and Carrot Mash

- Cook the swede and carrots together in a pan of boiling salted water for 30-35 minutes. Drain and return to the pan.
- Add the butter and garlic, mash well and season with salt and pepper to taste.
- Fill the Yorkshire puddings with the cooked meat and veg, soak in gravy, and enjoy!

Lighter Bites & Sides

Club Sandwich
Chicken Caesar Salad
Mini Chicken Kievs
Breakfast Crumpet Stack
Cheesy Chilli Dip
Tuna, Broccoli, Pasta Salad
Prawn Salad Spoons
Savoury Salmon Cheesecakes
Salmon Fishcakes
Cheese & Onion Quiche
Mini Feta and Broccoli Quiches
Sweetcorn Fritters
Cheese Scones
Cauliflower & Broccoli Cheese
Air fryer Chips
Smashed Peas
Mushroom Pâté
Sweet Chilli Hummus
Curry Paste

Lighter Bites & Sides

Club Sandwich

Serving Size: 2

Ingredients

4 slices white toastie bread, buttered

2 tbsp shop-bought rainbow coleslaw, finely chopped

2 Iceberg lettuce leaves
(Iceberg lettuce has a lower fibre content than other lettuce types, making it easier to digest)

1 tomato, thinly sliced

1 tbsp mayonnaise

150g packet shop-bought cooked roast chicken, sliced

2 thick cut bacon rashers, cooked

1 tbsp grated cheddar cheese

Chopped fresh parsley to garnish

Frozen or homemade potato wedges, tomato ketchup and mayonnaise to serve

- Heat a griddle pan over a high heat. Place the bread, butter side down, and heat until toasted. Flip and toast the other side.
- Spread 1 tbsp coleslaw on the first slice of bread. Add a lettuce leaf and tomato.
- Place the second slice of bread on top and spread a layer of mayonnaise over it. Add the chicken and bacon.
- Place the third slice of bread on top, spread the remaining coleslaw, sprinkle on the grated cheese, add the second lettuce leaf and top with the last slice of bread.
- Insert 4 wooden skewers in the middle of the straight edges. Using a sharp bread knife, cut the club sandwich diagonally into 4 triangles.
- Arrange on a serving plate with the cooked potato wedges, tomato ketchup and mayonnaise. Enjoy!

Lighter Bites & Sides

Chicken Caesar Salad

Serving Size: 4

Ingredients

1 small ciabatta loaf
2 tbsp olive oil
3 skinless, boneless chicken breasts
½ Iceberg lettuce, finely shredded *(Iceberg lettuce has a lower fibre content than other lettuce types, making it easier to digest)*
1 garlic clove, minced
1 anchovy fillet, mashed with a fork
Parmesan cheese for grating and shaving
5 tbsp mayonnaise
1 tsp Dijon mustard
1 tbsp white wine vinegar
Freshly ground salt and pepper to taste

- Heat oven to 200°C / gas 6. Tear or cut the ciabatta into chunks (croutons). Spread across a large baking sheet and drizzle with 2 tbsp olive oil. Toss to evenly coat. Sprinkle with some freshly ground sea salt.
- Bake in the oven for 8-10 minutes, turning the croutons a few times during baking so they brown evenly. Alternatively, place in the air fryer at 180°C and cook for about 5 minutes, checking and shaking them regularly.
- Rub the chicken breasts with 1 tbsp olive oil and season with salt and pepper. Place a pan over a medium heat for 1 minute, until hot. Place the chicken in the pan and cook for 4 minutes. Turn the chicken over and cook for another 4 minutes, or until cooked through.
- Mix the garlic and anchovies together in a small bowl. Grate a handful of Parmesan cheese and mix with the garlic, anchovies, mayonnaise, Dijon mustard and white wine vinegar. Season with salt and pepper to taste.
- Shave the Parmesan with a peeler. Add the shredded lettuce to one large or 4 small bowls. Pull the chicken into bite-size pieces with 2 forks. Scatter half over the leaves, along with half of the croutons.
- Add most of the dressing, then the rest of the chicken and croutons. Drizzle with the remaining dressing. Scatter the Parmesan shavings on top, and enjoy!

Lighter Bites & Sides

Mini Chicken Kievs

Serving Size: makes 12

Ingredients

2 garlic cloves, minced
1 tbsp fresh parsley, finely chopped
1 vegetable stock pot
¼ tsp onion granules
90g unsalted butter, softened

400g chicken mince
¼ tsp onion granules
1 tbsp fresh parsley, finely chopped

Freshly ground salt and pepper
50g breadcrumbs
2 tbsp cornflour
1 egg, beaten

Salad to serve

- Place the garlic, parsley, stock pot, onion granules and butter into a food processor, and pulse until combined. Line a tray with non-stick paper, then with a melon baller *(if you have one, if not, a teaspoon will do)* scoop out 12 balls of the mixture and place on the tray, making sure they do not touch each other. Place the tray into the freezer for about 30 minutes.
- In a large bowl, mix together the chicken mince, onion granules, parsley and salt and pepper to taste.
- Pre-heat the oven to 200ºC / gas 6. Remove the filling from the freezer. Take a tbsp amount of chicken mince and, with clean hands, encase the frozen filling with the chicken. Gently roll with your hands to make a small ball.
- Prepare 3 bowls: one with the cornflour, one with egg and one with breadcrumbs. Roll the balls into the cornflour, egg and then the breadcrumbs. Place the balls onto a lined baking tray and cook on the middle shelf for 25 minutes, or until cooked through and golden brown, turning halfway through. Serve with salad or as a tapas dish, and enjoy!

Lighter Bites & Sides

Breakfast Crumpet Stack

Serving Size: 4

Ingredients

4 hash browns
1 beef tomato, thinly sliced into 4
1 tbsp olive oil
4 sausages (or 350g pork sausage meat)

4 free range large eggs
8 crumpet thins
4 slices back bacon, thick cut

- Pre-heat air fryer to 190ºC and set to 25 minutes. Add the hash browns. Cook for 10 minutes. Then remove the basket, flip the hash browns over and add the slices of beef tomato to the basket on baking paper. Continue cooking for the remaining time. *Alternatively, cook in a pre-heated oven 200ºC / gas 7.*
- Whilst the hash browns are cooking, divide the sausage meat into 4, or slice the sausage skins and remove the meat, discarding the skins. Using clean hands, make 4 round patties to the size of the crumpets.
- Heat a large frying pan to a medium heat, add the oil and fry the sausage meat and bacon slices for 3-4 minutes each side or until cooked through.
- Transfer to a warm plate to rest. Using the same pan, fry the eggs to your liking.
- Toast the crumpets under the grill or in a toaster. Once done, build the stacks first by buttering the crumpets, then adding a squirt of your favourite sauce (brown sauce for me). Layer up with the sausage patty, tomato slice, bacon, hash brown and fried egg. Top with the other buttered crumpet, and enjoy!

Lighter Bites & Sides

Cheesy Chilli Dip

Serving Size: 2

Ingredients

1 tin 400g chilli con carne
115g cream cheese
1 tsp chilli powder
1 garlic clove, minced
115g mature cheddar, grated
Chopped fresh chilli *(optional)*

½ tomato, finely diced
Fresh parsley, chopped

Tortilla chips to serve

- Pre-heat oven to 180ºC / gas 4.
- Tip the tin of chilli con carne into a food processor and lightly pulse, until all the kidney beans have been chopped up into small pieces.
- Combine cream cheese, chilli powder and optional fresh chilli. Mix well.
- Mix in the grated cheese and garlic.
- Place mixture into a small baker and spread evenly with the back of a spoon.
- Bake for 20-25 minutes, stirring twice throughout.
- Remove from the oven, allow to cool a little, garnish with tomato and parsley.
- Service with tortilla chips, and enjoy!

Lighter Bites & Sides

Tuna, Broccoli, Pasta Salad

Serving Size: 4

Ingredients

1 tbsp olive oil
200g tenderstem broccoli
1 garlic clove, minced
½ tsp dried crushed chilli flakes

350g dried fusilli pasta
145g tin tuna chunks, drained

- Heat the oil in a pan over a medium heat. Chop the broccoli into small florets. Stir fry the broccoli, garlic and chilli flakes for a few minutes. Set aside to cool.
- In a large pan of lightly salted boiling water, cook the pasta according to packet instructions. Once cooked, run under cold water, drain and tip into a serving bowl.
- Flake the tuna into the pasta, add the broccoli, garlic and chilli flakes. Mix well, and enjoy!

Lighter Bites & Sides

Prawn Salad Spoons

Serving Size: 2

Ingredients

8-10 cooked, peeled prawns
2 tbsp mayonnaise
1 tbsp sweet chilli sauce
1 tsp spring onion, very finely chopped
¼ tsp garlic granules
1 Iceberg lettuce leaf, very finely sliced
Pinch paprika

4 small sprigs dill, to garnish

Note:
For a larger starter or snack, use double the ingredients and layer up in individual dessert glasses.

- Defrost the prawns, if using frozen.
- Mix the mayonnaise, sweet chilli sauce, spring onion and garlic granules in a small bowl.
- Reserve 2 whole prawns. Chop the rest into small pieces and stir into the mayo mix. Sprinkle a little finely sliced lettuce onto 4 spoons (I use Chinese soup spoons) and add a spoonful of the prawn mixture to each.
- Slice the 2 remaining prawns in half lengthways and place on top of each spoon. Sprinkle with paprika and garnish with a sprig of dill. Enjoy!

Lighter Bites & Sides

Savoury Salmon Cheesecakes

Serving Size: 2

Ingredients

55g savoury crackers
Good handful of rocket salad
25g unsalted butter
165g cream cheese
50g smoked salmon

1 tbsp snipped chives
salt and pepper to taste
Zest of ½ lemon
Few sprigs of fresh dill

- Blitz crackers and rocket in a food processor.
- Melt the butter in a bowl and add to the biscuit mixture. Mix well.
- Divide the crust between two 7-10cm moulds, making sure to press it down well with the back of a spoon.
- Mix the cream cheese, 30g chopped salmon, chives and lemon zest, then top the crust with cheese mixture. Chill in the fridge for 15 minutes.
- Remove from the mould. Garnish the cheesecake with the remaining salmon and dill. Enjoy!

Lighter Bites & Sides

Salmon Fishcakes

Serving Size: 4

Ingredients

1 large potato, peeled and cubed
Olive oil
2 boneless salmon fillets
Freshly ground salt and pepper
1 tbsp plain flour + extra for dusting

2 spring onions, finely sliced
Zest of ½ lemon
Fresh parsley, chopped

Lemon and tartare sauce to serve

- In the bottom pan of a hob steamer, boil the potato in lightly salted water for 8-10 minutes.
- Lightly oil the salmon fillets, season with salt and pepper, then add to the steamer above the potato. Place the lid on, turn the heat down to low and steam for 8-10 minutes, or until the salmon is cooked.
- Transfer the salmon to a plate. Drain the potatoes and let steam dry for a minute, then mash the potatoes and allow to cool for a few minutes.
- Flake the salmon into the mash with 1 tbsp flour, the spring onions, lemon zest and parsley. Season with salt and pepper to taste. Mix until combined.
- Divide into 4, then with clean hands, shape into round cakes about 2cm thick, dusting with flour as you go. Place onto a plate and chill in the fridge for 30 minutes.
- Heat 2 tbsp oil in a large pan over a medium-high heat. Add the fishcakes and fry for 3-4 minutes on each side, or until crisp and golden.
- Serve with tartare sauce, plus a lemon wedge, and enjoy!

Lighter Bites & Sides

Cheese & Onion Quiche

Serving Size: 8

Ingredients

1 tbsp olive oil, + extra for tin
Plain flour for dusting
320g pack ready rolled short-crust pastry
1 white onion, very finely chopped
Large bunch spring onions, very finely sliced

4 eggs, + 1 egg yolk
200ml whole milk
50ml double cream
Small bunch fresh chives, snipped
150g mature cheddar, grated

- Lightly grease a 23cm quiche dish/tin. Roll out the pastry into a circle that's bigger than the tin. Gently lay the pastry into the tin and press carefully into the base and sides. Leave any overhang over the sides of the tin. Chill in the fridge for 30 minutes.
- Heat the oil in a frying pan over a low-medium heat. Stir in the onion and fry gently for 15 minutes. Tip in the spring onions and fry for a few more minutes until softened. Take off the heat and leave to cool slightly.
- Heat the oven to 200°C / gas 6. Scrunch up a sheet of baking paper and line the pastry, ensuring it goes over the edges. Fill with baking beans. Bake for 15-20 minutes.
- Remove the beans and paper. Bake for a further 5-10 minutes until lightly golden. Trim the pastry edges.
- While the pastry is baking, in a jug, whisk together the eggs, cream, milk and chives. Season well with salt and black pepper.
- Reduce oven temperature to 180°C / gas 4. Place the quiche tin on a baking sheet and scatter the onions evenly over the base. Sprinkle over most of the grated cheddar and pour the egg mixture over. Top with the rest of the cheese and bake for 25-30 minutes, until set and lightly golden.
- Remove from the oven and allow to cool for 10-15 minutes before slicing. Enjoy!

Lighter Bites & Sides

Mini Feta and Broccoli Quiches

Serving Size: 6

Ingredients

150g tenderstem broccoli, chopped *(discard stems)*
Good knob of butter
3-4 spring onions, finely sliced
1 garlic clove, finely minced

Pack ready-rolled shortcrust pastry
3 medium eggs, + 1 egg yolk
150g single cream
1 tbsp fresh chives, snipped
100g feta cheese

- Pre-heat the oven to 200ºC / gas 6.
- Heat a large frying pan. Add the butter and gently fry the broccoli, spring onions and garlic for a few minutes. Remove from the heat and set aside.
- Unroll the pastry on its paper. Cut out rounds of pastry using a 10cm pastry cutter, then gently push them into the wells of a 6-hold muffin tray. Prick each base with a fork.
- Place paper muffin cases inside each well, fill with baking beans and blind bake for 15 minutes, removing the paper for the final 5 minutes.
- Whisk the eggs, yolk and cream in a jug. Add the snipped chives. Season with salt and pepper to taste.
- Divide the broccoli, spring onions and garlic mixture evenly into each pastry case, top with the eggs and cream, and crumble the feta over. Cook on the middle shelf for 15 minutes, or until slightly browned and just set.
- Serve hot or cold, and enjoy!

Lighter Bites & Sides

Sweetcorn Fritters

Serving Size: 8

Ingredients

2x 200g tins sweetcorn
125g self-raising flour
1 tsp baking powder
1 tsp smoked paprika
140ml full fat milk
1 egg, beaten
1 tbsp fresh chives, snipped
Handful of parsley, chopped

2 spring onions, finely sliced
Freshly ground salt and black pepper
Rapeseed or vegetable oil for frying

Sweet chilli sauce to serve

- Drain the tins of sweetcorn, then tip into a food processor. Pulse until no whole corns remain.
- In a large bowl, mix the flour, baking powder, paprika, milk and egg until smooth. Add the sweetcorn, chives, parsley and spring onions. Season with salt and pepper, and mix well.
- In a large frying pan, heat about 1cm of oil over a medium-high heat. Spoon 2 tablespoons of the mixture into the pan and fry for 2-3 minutes each side, or until golden and crispy.
- Remove from the pan and place on some kitchen roll to drain.
- Serve while still hot with sweet chilli dipping sauce. Enjoy!

Lighter Bites & Sides

Cheese Scones
Serving Size: 8

Ingredients

350g self-raising flour
2 tsp baking powder
85g grated cold butter
1 egg, beaten
Juice of ½ lemon
2-3 tbsp grated cheddar
1 tsp paprika or mustard powder

Splash of milk, more as required
Egg wash (egg with a little water or milk) and grated cheese to top

Butter to serve

- Pre-heat a pizza stone – if you have one – to 220°C / gas 7 on middle shelf. If not, a large baking tray will do.
- Sift the flour and baking powder into a large bowl.
- Add the butter, egg, cheese, lemon juice and paprika or mustard powder, and mix gently to form a loose dough. Add milk, if needed, to make a dryish dough.
- On a floured surface, make a round disc out of the dough (it will be a little crumbly).
- Take the pizza stone/baking tray out of the oven and place the dough disc on it. Cut into 8 triangles, moving them apart from each other.
- Brush with egg wash and sprinkle some grated cheese over each triangle.
- Pop in the oven and turn down to 200°C / gas 6. Bake for 20 minutes.
- Remove from the oven and let cool slightly on the stone/tray.
- Whilst still warm, spread with plenty of butter, and enjoy!

Lighter Bites & Sides

Cauliflower & Broccoli Cheese

Serving Size: 6

Ingredients

1 small cauliflower, cut into small florets
1 small head broccoli, cut into small florets
50g butter
1 garlic clove, minced
50g flour

500ml full fat milk
100g grated mature cheddar
1 heaped tsp Dijon mustard
1 tbsp finely snipped chives
Salt and pepper to taste.

- Pre-heat oven to 200°C / gas 6.
- In a large saucepan, cook the cauliflower in boiling salted water for 5 minutes, then add the broccoli and cook for a further 3 minutes. Take off the heat, drain well and leave to steam dry.
- Melt the butter in a pan over a medium heat. Add the garlic and heat for 30 seconds before adding the flour. Cook for 1 minute, stirring constantly.
- A little at a time, add the milk, stirring constantly. Bring to a boil, then turn the heat down and simmer for 2 minutes, until thickened.
- Take the sauce off the heat and stir through most of the cheese, Dijon mustard and chives. Season to taste.
- Mix the cauliflower and broccoli into the sauce. Spoon into a large ovenproof dish. Sprinkle the rest of the cheese over the top and cook in the oven for 30-35 minutes, until the cheese is bubbling and golden.
- Leave to rest for 5 minutes before serving, and enjoy!

Lighter Bites & Sides

Air Fryer Chips

Ingredients

650g floury potatoes such as Maris Piper or Rooster, peeled and sliced into chips
1 tbsp cornflour
2 tbsp rapeseed, sunflower or vegetable oil

1 tsp salt
½ tsp freshly ground pepper
½ tsp paprika

Condiments to serve

- Peel and chop the potatoes into chips, around 1cm thick. Soak in cold water for about 15 minutes. Rinse with more cold water. Drain and pat dry with kitchen paper or a clean tea towel.
- In a large bowl, toss the chips with the cornflour until coated. Add the oil, salt, pepper and paprika. Toss again so the chips are evenly coated.
- Place the chips into the air fryer basket and cook at 190ºC for about 20 minutes, shaking every few minutes, until deliciously crispy.
- Serve with another grind of salt and your favourite condiments. Enjoy!

Lighter Bites & Sides

Smashed Peas

Serving Size: 2

Ingredients

2 tbsp olive oil
200g frozen peas, defrosted
3 spring onions, finely sliced
Small handful fresh mint leaves, finely chopped

Good knob of butter
Salt and pepper to taste

- Heat the oil in a small pan over a medium heat.
- Add the spring onions and peas. Cook for about 5-6 minutes, stirring frequently. Add the chopped mint leaves. Continue to cook for another couple of minutes, stirring frequently.
- Transfer to a bowl and mash until peas are crushed to your liking. Add the butter, salt and pepper. Stir until the butter has melted. Enjoy!

Lighter Bites & Sides

Mushroom Pâté

Serving Size: 6

Ingredients

25g dried porcini mushrooms
500g chestnut mushrooms, roughly chopped
125g shiitake mushrooms, roughly chopped
2 tbsp peanut oil
Freshly ground sea salt
½ red onion, finely chopped
3 garlic cloves, minced
1 tsp dried thyme
50ml port
200g full fat cream cheese
Freshly ground black pepper

Crackers or toasted bread to serve

- Put the dried mushrooms into a bowl, cover with boiling water and leave to stand.
- Place the chestnut and shiitake mushrooms into a food processor and pulse until finely chopped.
- Heat a large frying pan over a medium-high heat. Add 1 tbsp of the oil and the finely chopped mushrooms, with a pinch of salt. Fry, stirring frequently for 10 minutes until the liquid has evaporated and the mushrooms start to caramelise. Remove from the heat and spoon back into the food processor.
- Heat the remaining oil in the same pan, and add the onion with a pinch of salt. Fry for 5 minutes until softened, then add the garlic and thyme. Cook for another minute, then pour in the port.
- Drain the porcini mushrooms, keeping 50ml of the liquid. Finely chop the mushrooms and add to the pan with the liquid. Simmer, stirring, until almost all of the liquid has evaporated. Remove from the heat and allow to cool for 5-10 minutes, then spoon into the food processor with the other mushrooms.
- Add the cream cheese to the food processor, season with freshly ground pepper and pulse everything to a smooth pâté.
- Scoop into 6 small serving dishes, and enjoy!

Lighter Bites & Sides

Sweet Chilli Hummus

Ingredients

400g tin chickpeas, drained and rinsed well
2 cloves garlic, minced
1 tbsp extra virgin olive oil
1 tbsp Tahini or smooth peanut butter
½ tsp sesame oil
¼ tsp paprika
1 tbsp hot water
1 tbsp sweet chilli sauce

Good squeeze lemon juice
Salt and freshly ground black pepper

Notes:
Swap the sweet chilli sauce for either beetroot, avocado, roasted red peppers etc.
Be adventurous and experiment.

- Place all the ingredients (except the lemon juice and pepper) into a food processor or blender. Pulse for 30 seconds then stop and scrape down the sides with a rubber spatula.
- Add a squirt of lemon juice then repeat at least 3 more times, or until the hummus is thick, yet smooth. Add salt and pepper to taste.
- If you want a smoother, less thick hummus, add another tablespoon of hot water at this point.
- Give the hummus one last good blitz, transfer to a serving bowl, drizzle a little sweet chilli sauce on top, and enjoy!

Lighter Bites & Sides

Curry Paste

Ingredients

- 2 tbsp cumin seeds
- 2 tbsp coriander seeds
- 1 tsp fennel seeds
- 1 tbsp mustard seeds
- 1 tsp black peppercorns
- 2 tsp paprika
- 1 tsp ground turmeric
- 1 tsp ground cinnamon
- 1-2 dried chillies
- 1 tsp salt
- 3 garlic cloves, minced
- ½ tbsp fresh ginger, grated
- 1 tbsp tomato purée
- 4 tbsp white wine vinegar

- Heat a dry frying pan over a medium heat. Add the seeds and peppercorns and cook for 2-3 minutes, stirring until golden in colour. Allow to cool for a few minutes.
- Add the paprika, turmeric, cinnamon, dried chillies and salt to a pestle and mortar. Add the cooled seeds, then grind to a fine powder.
- Mix in the garlic, ginger, tomato purée and vinegar. Mix well to make a paste.
- Use in your favourite recipes, and enjoy!

It is estimated that 176,000 to 205,000 people are living with a Stoma in the UK, and over 13 million worldwide

For Afters

Sticky Toffee Pudding
Microwave Jam Sponge Puddings
Apple Caramel Crumble
Biscoff Cheesecake Pots
Berry Crumble
Banoffee Pots
Pistachio and White Chocolate Cheesecake
Rocky Road
Carrot Cake

For Afters

Sticky Toffee Pudding

Serving Size: 12

Ingredients

Sponge
250ml boiling water
300g dates, chopped well
3 tbsp instant coffee powder
1 tsp bicarbonate of soda
1 tsp vanilla extract
150 g butter
250g caster sugar
3 eggs

300g self raising flour

Toffee
25g unsalted butter
200g soft brown sugar
100ml double cream

Cream or ice cream to serve

- Pour 250ml boiling water over the dates, coffee and bicarbonate of soda and set aside to soak for 10 minutes. Add the vanilla extract and mash the mixture well with a fork.
- Pre-heat oven to 180°C / gas 4. Lightly butter a 10x8 inch (25x20cm) tin or ceramic dish.
- Beat the butter and sugar with a wooden spoon until smooth. Whisk the eggs and add to the mixture, followed by the date mix. Fold in the flour and combine well.
- Bake for 45 to 50 minutes on the middle shelf.

Toffee

- Over a low heat, melt the butter, sugar and cream in a small pan. Gently bubble for 2-3 minutes.
- As soon as the cake is out of the oven, prick all over with a cocktail stick and pour the toffee over the top.
- Cut into squares and serve with fresh cream or ice cream, and enjoy!

Notes: If there are any leftovers, the pudding freezes well.

For Afters

Microwave Jam Sponge Puddings

Serving Size: 4

Ingredients

Sponge
120g butter or margarine, + a little extra to grease the bowls
4 tbsp seedless raspberry jam
120g caster sugar
2 medium eggs, beaten
1 tsp vanilla extract
120g self raising flour

Custard, cream or ice cream to serve

- Grease 4 small microwaveable bowls with butter.
- Spoon 1 tbsp jam into each of the greased bowls. Set aside.
- In a large mixing bowl, cream together the butter and caster sugar until light and fluffy. Mix in the eggs and vanilla extract. Tip in the flour and mix together until combined.
- Spoon the batter into the bowls on top of the jam. Microwave on full power for 5 minutes.
- Carefully remove from the microwave and let rest for a minute. Run a knife around the edge of the bowls to loosen the puddings, then turn out onto your serving plates/bowls.
- Serve with custard, cream or ice cream, and enjoy!

For Afters

Apple Caramel Crumble

Serving Size: 4

Ingredients

3-4 medium Bramley apples, peeled, cored and cut into 1cm pieces
2 tbsp golden caster sugar
1 tin Carnation caramel

150g plain flour
100g golden caster sugar
100g cold butter, cut into cubes

Custard, cream or ice cream to serve

- Heat oven to 190°C / gas 5.
- Mix the chopped apples with 2 tbsp sugar and divide between 4 individual ovenproof dishes.
- Open the tin of caramel and give it a stir to loosen the contents. Drizzle half the tin over the apples.
- In a large bowl rub the flour, sugar and butter with your fingers until it looks like moist breadcrumbs. Alternatively, pulse in a food processor.
- Cover the apple mixture with the crumble and cook in the oven for 20-30 minutes, until the crumble is golden.
- Remove from the oven, then drizzle another spoonful of the caramel over the top.
- Serve with custard, cream or ice cream, and enjoy!

For Afters

Biscoff Cheesecake Pots

Serving Size: 12

Ingredients

200g Biscoff biscuits
50g unsalted butter, melted

400g cream cheese
75g soft brown sugar
150g Biscoff spread
1tsp vanilla extract
200g double cream

100g Biscoff spread, melted
Whipped double cream

- Place the biscuits into a food processor and pulse until fine crumbs (set aside a handful for serving). Gently heat butter in the microwave in short bursts until the butter is melted. Stir in the crushed biscuits and mix until combined. Divide between 12 small plastic cups or glasses, and press down until firm. Chill in the fridge.
- Put the cream cheese and sugar into a large bowl and mix together until smooth. Add 150g Biscoff spread and the vanilla. Mix until combined.
- Slowly pour in the cream while whisking with an electric hand whisk. Keep whisking until the mixture is thick.
- Spoon the mixture into a large piping bag and top the biscuit bases, leaving an inch or so free at the top of the cups. Gently tap cups on the work surface to level them off. Place in the fridge for 30 minutes.
- Spoon 100g Biscoff spread into a small jug. Heat in the microwave on short bursts to melt the spread. Stir in between bursts until the spread has melted. Pour the melted spread over the cheesecake filling almost to the top of the cups.
- Pipe a swirl of whipped cream onto each cheesecake and finish with a sprinkle of the reserved Biscoff crumbs. Enjoy!

For Afters

Berry Crumble

Serving Size: 4

Ingredients

250g frozen Black Forest berries, defrosted
2 tbsp golden caster sugar

150g plain flour
100g golden caster sugar
100g cold butter, cut into cubes

Custard, cream or ice cream to serve

- Pre-heat oven to 190°C / gas 5.
- Once the fruit has defrosted, tip into a food processor and pulse until chopped into small pieces.
- Mix the fruit with the sugar and place in a 7 inch (18cm) round oven-proof dish.
- With your fingers, rub the flour, sugar and butter in a large bowl until it all looks like moist breadcrumbs. Alternatively, pulse in a food processor.
- Cover the fruit mixture with the crumble and bake in the oven for 20-30 minutes, until the crumble is golden.
- Remove from the oven, leave to cool for a few minutes. Serve with custard, cream or ice cream, and enjoy!

For Afters

Banoffee Pots

Serving Size: 4

Ingredients

8 digestive biscuits, crushed
25g unsalted butter, melted
4 tbsp caramel sauce

4 bananas, sliced
250ml double cream, whipped
Grated chocolate

- Place the biscuits into a food processor and blitz until they're fine crumbs. Tip into the melted butter and mix well.
- Divide the biscuit mixture between 4 small dessert dishes or glasses. Firm down with the back of a spoon.
- Layer the sliced bananas on top, reserving some slices for garnish. Drizzle the caramel sauce over, then pipe the cream on top.
- Add a few slices of banana, sprinkle with grated chocolate, and enjoy!

For Afters

Pistachio and White Chocolate Cheesecake

Serving Size: 12

Ingredients

300g digestive biscuits
150g unsalted butter, melted

300g white chocolate
400g full fat cream cheese
75g icing sugar
300ml double cream

125g shelled, unsalted pistachios, chopped into very small pieces *(I use a hand chopper)*

50ml double cream
1 tbsp icing sugar

- Blitz the digestive biscuits in a food processor.
- Add the melted butter and mix well.
- Tip the biscuit mixture into the bottom of a deep 20cm (8in) loose bottom tin and press down firmly. Set aside.
- Melt the white chocolate in a bowl over a pan of simmering water, or in the microwave on short bursts, until fully melted. Leave to cool slightly.
- Mix the cream cheese with 75g icing sugar until smooth. Add 300ml double cream and continue to whisk until you have soft peaks.
- Fold in your cooled melted chocolate and approximately 100g chopped pistachios (reserving 25g or so for decoration).
- Spread the mix over the biscuit base, smooth and chill in the fridge for at least 4 to 5 hours, or overnight.
- Remove from tin and place on a serving plate.
- Whisk 50ml cream and 1 tbsp icing sugar. Pipe swirls on top and sprinkle the remaining finely chopped pistachios over the top. Enjoy!

For Afters

Rocky Road

Serving Size: 25 small bites

Ingredients

100g dark chocolate
200g milk chocolate with caramel filling
5 digestive biscuits, roughly broken up
Good handful Maltesers, roughly broken up
Handful almonds, chopped into small pieces
Handful dried cranberries, finely chopped

- Melt the chocolate in a large bowl by placing in the microwave and heating on short bursts of 30 seconds. Mix each time until mostly melted, with just a few lumps intact.
- Mix the biscuits, Maltesers, nuts and cranberries into the melted chocolate.
- Spread the mixture into a shallow cake or brownie tin, and smooth over with the back of a spoon. Place in the fridge for 30 minutes.
- Remove from the fridge, cut into bitesize pieces (or bigger if you want) and enjoy!

For Afters

Carrot Cake
Serving Size: 12

Ingredients

150ml sunflower oil
225g self-raising flour
1 tsp baking powder
1½ tsp cinnamon
½ tsp mixed spice
½ tsp ground ginger
225g light brown sugar
Zest of ½ an orange, finely grated
100g pecans, chopped into very small pieces (reserve some to sprinkle on top)
250g carrots, grated
3 medium eggs, beaten

For the icing
50 g butter, softened
200g full-fat cream cheese
100g icing sugar
Zest of ½ an orange, finely grated

Notes:
Try swapping the carrots for parsnips – sounds strange, but tastes amazing!

- Pre-heat oven to 180°C / gas 4. Grease two 18cm loose-bottomed round cake tins and line with baking paper.
- Sift the flour, baking powder, mixed spice, cinnamon and ginger into a large bowl. Add the light brown sugar, zest of ½ an orange, pecans (keep some to sprinkle on top) and grated carrots. Stir until well combined.
- Pour in the beaten eggs and oil. Mix well.
- Divide the mixture between the prepared cake tins. Bake in the oven, on the middle shelf, for 45 minutes to an hour, or until a skewer comes out clean. Remove from the oven, cool on a rack until cool enough to handle. Turn out and leave to cool completely before icing.

Icing

- Whisk the butter in a large bowl with an electric hand mixer until soft. Add the cream cheese and whisk until combined. Sift in the icing sugar, add most of the remaining ½ orange zest (reserving some to sprinkle over the top), and mix until smooth.
- To make one large cake, sandwich together the 2 cakes with half the icing. Spread the remaining icing over the top, sprinkle with the reserved pecan nuts and zest. Alternatively, make 2 smaller cakes by adding the icing to just the top of the cakes. Sprinkle with pecan nuts and zest, and enjoy!

Acknowledgements

Special Thanks
Serving Size: All

Ingredients

- Hard work
- Lots of support
- Guidance
- Advice
- Blood
- Sweat
- And Tears

- Special thanks to my family and friends who have supported me and helped make this cookbook a reality.
- Huge thanks to my amazing Mum, who is most probably my biggest fan.
- My Mother and Father-in-law for handing down recipes, and pushing me forward to make my ideas happen.
- I am so appreciative of the support and advice from my children, Ethan and Kasey, also their partners Ellie and Tyler.
- I am immensely grateful to my taste testers, for their constructive feedback and enthusiasm, especially my husband Graham.
- I can't thank my stoma nurses enough for their care and advice, from 26 years ago, to this day.
- Massive thank you to Hannah, for believing in me, encouraging me and the never ending support you give.
- Julie, Sarah, Amy, Jamie and Hazel, thank you for your advice, your patience, guidance and for listening to me talk constantly about my recipes and food.
- And finally, I am deeply grateful to my publisher, Intoprint, Mark and Anne Webb and their team, for the unwavering support and belief in this project. Your expertise and dedication have been invaluable, and I am incredibly grateful for your professionalism and collaboration throughout this journey.

www.ingramcontent.com/pod-product-compliance
Lightning Source LLC
Chambersburg PA
CBHW040313170426
43195CB00020B/2955